When boredom strikes,
And time seems slow,
Your parents are busy,
And there's nowhere to go,

Go get this fun book,
Right off the shelf,
It is full of adventures,
You can do by yourself!

Flip through it's pages,
You'll find many things to do.
Like draw a picture, do a puzzle or
Build a fort, to name a few.

Ride your bike,
Make paper airplanes,
Listen to music or
Play outdoors,

For in this book,
Between it's covers,
Boredom fades and
Adventure roars!

ISBN 979-8-9902790-0-1

©2024 Kenny Kiskis

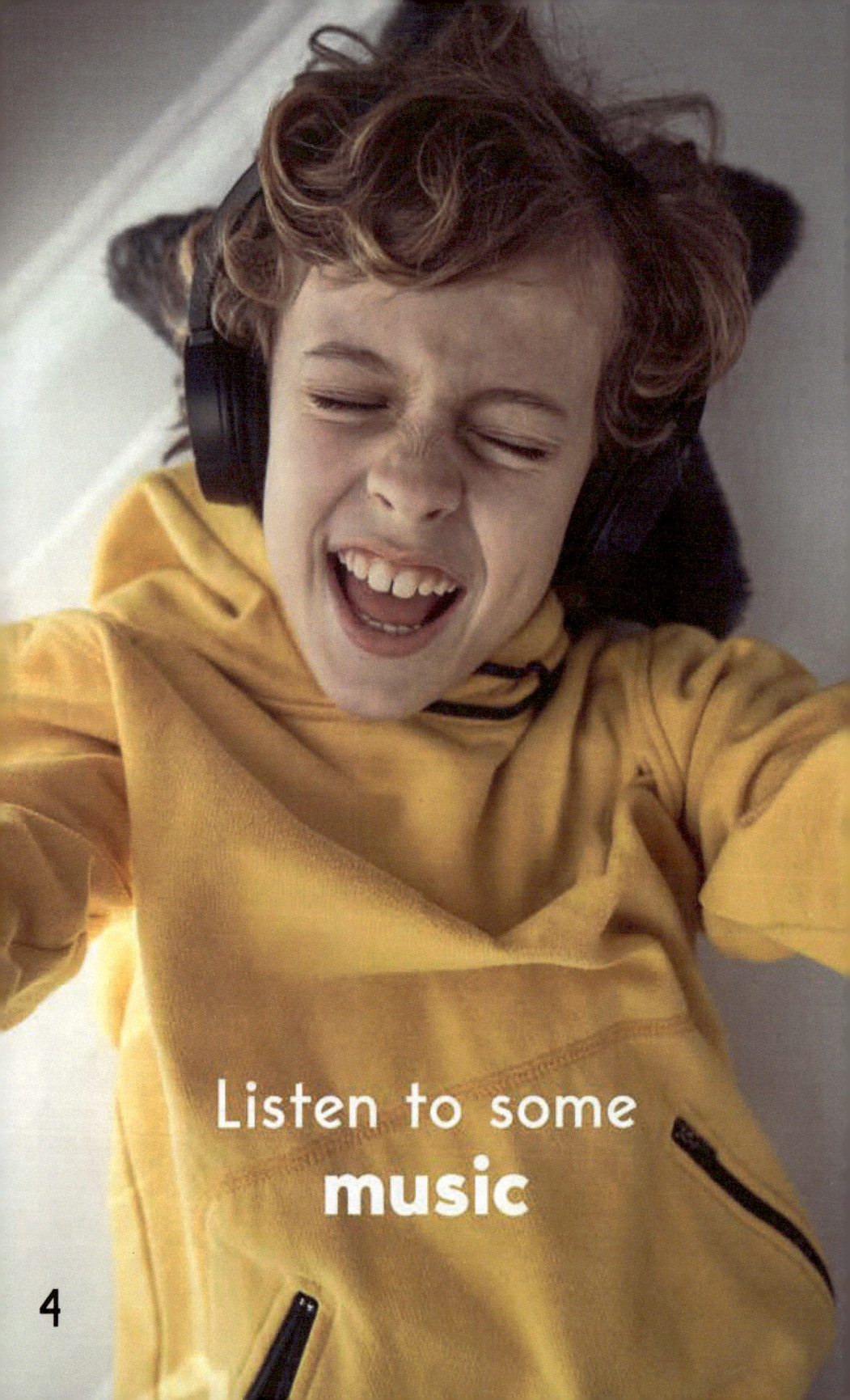

Paint a **picture**

Ride a bicycle

Make friendship bracelets

Build a **fort**

Explore **outside**

Play with **blocks**

Have a picnic with **healthy snacks**

Play **ball**

Read a book

Kenny Kiskis is a multifaceted individual, best known as the author of "Word's Don't Stick," a compelling guide empowering children to overcome name-calling and cultivate resilience. Through his work, Kiskis offers invaluable insights into fostering tough-love development in children.

His passion for empowering parents led him to write "It's OK to say Go Play," a tough love guide that emphasizes the importance of independent play in children's cognitive growth. Kiskis firmly believes in the power of play for nurturing creativity and problem-solving skills in young minds.

Beyond his contributions to parenting literature, Kenny Kiskis is an entrepreneur and business owner. He founded PrivacyShields.com, a company dedicated to improving student test scores, as well as SearchBarTees.com, which offers customized hilarious apparel.

With a blend of entrepreneurial spirit and a commitment to fostering healthy child development, Kenny Kiskis continues to make a meaningful impact in both the business and parenting realm

"It's OK to Say Go Play," by Kenny Kiskis, the author of "Word's Don't Stick," emphasizes the importance of independent play for children. It challenges the notion that telling children to "go play" is simply a way for parents to get some peace and quiet. Instead, the book argues that solo playtime is crucial for a child's development.

"It's OK to Say Go Play" uses illustrations and suggestions to showcase a variety of activities that children can engage in by themselves. The book highlights the benefits of independent play, showcasing how it fosters imagination, creativity, and even brain development. By encouraging children to play alone, the book empowers them to use their minds and explore their own ideas.

Ultimately, "It's OK to Say Go Play" offers a valuable perspective for both children and parents. It encourages children to embrace independent play and empowers parents to confidently allow their children the space and freedom to do so, knowing it contributes significantly to their well-being and development.

NOTES